FINDING WILDLIFE
in
COLORADO

Birds
Mammals
& Reptiles

Joe McDaniel

ISBN 978-1-950647-72-9

Published by BookCrafters, Parker, Colorado.
www.bookcrafters.net

BookCrafters

Table of Contents

Mammals
58

Reptiles
94

Introduction

Wildlife is plentiful in Colorado. At times our encounters can be brief and unexpected. Animals rarely wait for us to photograph them. Exploring Colorado means finding its wildlife; along highways or rural country roads, in residential neighborhoods and open spaces, or in the many Parks and Reserves set aside for its protection.

The animals shown in this book were photographed • in our neighborhood, • in our back yard, • out of our office window, • in the nearby Public Open Space where we walk regularly - along the Tallman Gulch Trail or • along rural country roads as we have explored Colorado's Parks, scenic and wildlife areas. The two mammal species noticeably absent from this collection are the Black Bear and the Mountain Lion. Our search for those continues!

In the Table of Contents I have listed each species alphabetically using the common name for each. For example, the American Avocet and the Golden Eagle are listed as *Avocet, American* and *Eagle, Golden* respectively. I have added a few brief notes on where the photos were taken.

• As a photographer I have learned the value of making adjustments to my camera *ahead of time* so that it is ready to use at a moment's notice. So, if it is dark, I adjust the ISO to allow for that quick shot that inevitably presents itself. As light conditions change, I take time to re-adjust the camera from time to time. Many of my best captures were made with just one or two brief shots when an animal unexpectedly appeared. If I had not had the camera close at hand, and already set correctly, I would have missed the opportunity altogether.

• When walking or driving — *look up*. Often when we are watching the ground for deer or turkeys, we will miss the hawk or the owl perched in a tree above us. Along highways and county roads the best place to find hawks and eagles is where they perch on utility or fence posts.

• *Be patient*. We can become frustrated after hours of searching for wildlife and seeing nothing. But that will often change in a moment and we will be rewarded with great sightings.

• *Caption your photographs*. There are excellent reference books available on birds, mammals, reptile and insects. Use the internet for research. Correct identification is important.

• *Share your successes*. There are many wildlife enthusiasts and photographers who, • take an interest in your successes, • can teach you, and • can learn from you. There are quite a few friendly social media sites where wildlife enthusiasts share photographs.

This is a collection of personal memories and experiences. It is most certainly not a book of outstanding wildlife photographs. My hope is that you can learn from it and enjoy it.

BIRDS

As of July 2020, 511 species of birds have been documented in Colorado.

Represented here are 46 birds species in 66 photographs.

WATCH
FOR
WILDLIFE

American Avocet

Red-winged Blackbird
Female

Red-winged Blackbird
Male

Buffelhead (Duck)

Black-capped Chickadee

Double-crested Cormorant

Prairie Falcon

Northern Flicker - Female

Flicker chicks

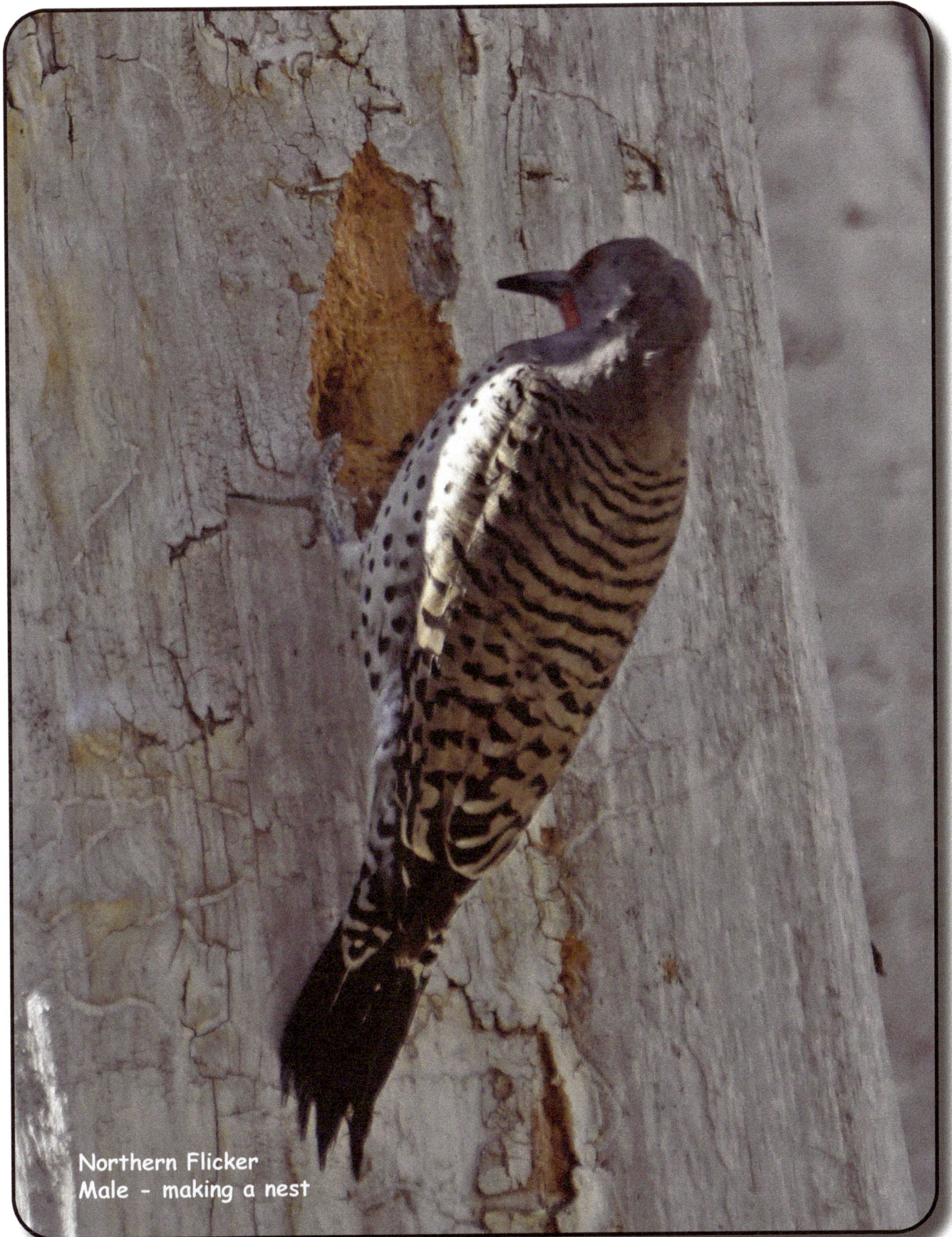

Northern Flicker
Male - making a nest

Blue Jay

Steller's Jay

11

Western Scrub Jay

Bald Eagle

13

Golden Eagle

Snowy Egret

Mourning Dove

Wood Duck - Female

Wood Duck - Male

House Finch - Male

Common Grackle

American Goldfinch

Canada Goose

Greater White-fronted Goose

Cooper's Hawk

Ferruginous Hawk

Red-tailed Hawk

Swainson's Hawks
Adult (top), Juvenile (bottom)

Swainson's Hawk

Swainson's Hawk

Black-crowned Night Heron

Great Blue Heron's Nest

Great Blue Heron

Broad-tailed Hummingbird

Broad-tailed Hummingbird

Killdeer

Black-billed Magpie

Mallard Hen & ducklings

Mallard Drake

Western Meadowlark

Western Meadowlark

Common Merganser

White-breasted Nuthatch

Bullock's Oriole

Osprey nest

Osprey

Great Horned Owl & chicks

Great Horned Owl

Great Horned Owl
Fledglings

American White Pelicans

American White Pelican

Ring-necked Pheasant
Female

Ring-necked Pheasant
Male

White-tailed Ptarmigan

48

Common Ravens

American Robin

Western Sandpiper

House Sparrows
Male (left) Female (right)

Barn Swallow

Barn Swallow
chicks

Tree Swallows

Cinnamon Teal

Spotted Towhee

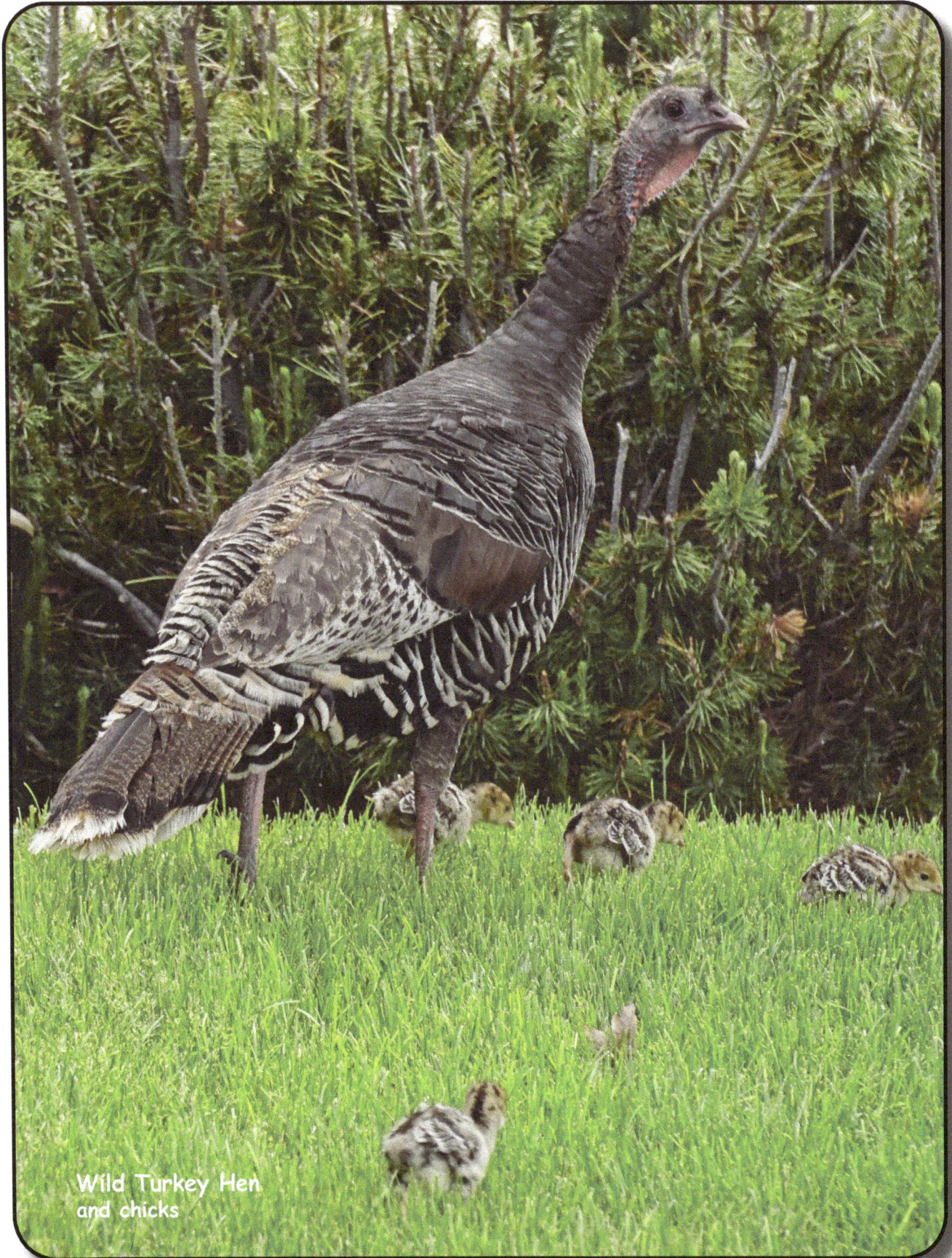

Wild Turkey Hen
and chicks

Wild Turkeys

Turkey Vulture

MAMMALS

18 Species of mammals are represented here in 37 photographs. The State Mammal of Colorado is the Bighorn Sheep - Pages 90 & 91.

SLOW DOWN
WILDLIFE CROSSING

BEAR RIGHT SLOW PLEASE

MARMOT XING

Pronghorn Antelope, Female
and twin fawns

Pronghorn Antelope, Male

59

American Beaver

American Bison, Bull

American Bison,
Cow and Calf

Bobcat

Least Chipmunk

Coyote, Female

Mule Deer, Buck

Mule Deer, Fawn
newborn

67

Mule Deer, Buck

Mule Deer, Fawn

Mule Deer Doe

Mule Deer, Doe (jumpimg) and fawn

This Mule Deer doe has a genetic
condition called *Leucism,* which
causes a partial loss of pigmentation.
It is not an albino, as many believe.

Mule Deer, Doe

White-tailed Deer, Buck

White-tailed Deer, Doe

Elk, Cow
(Wapiti)

Elk, Bull
(Wapiti)

Elk, Cows and Calves
(Wapiti)

'Red Fox' Kits

Red Fox

Rocky Mountain Goat

Rocky Mountain Goat

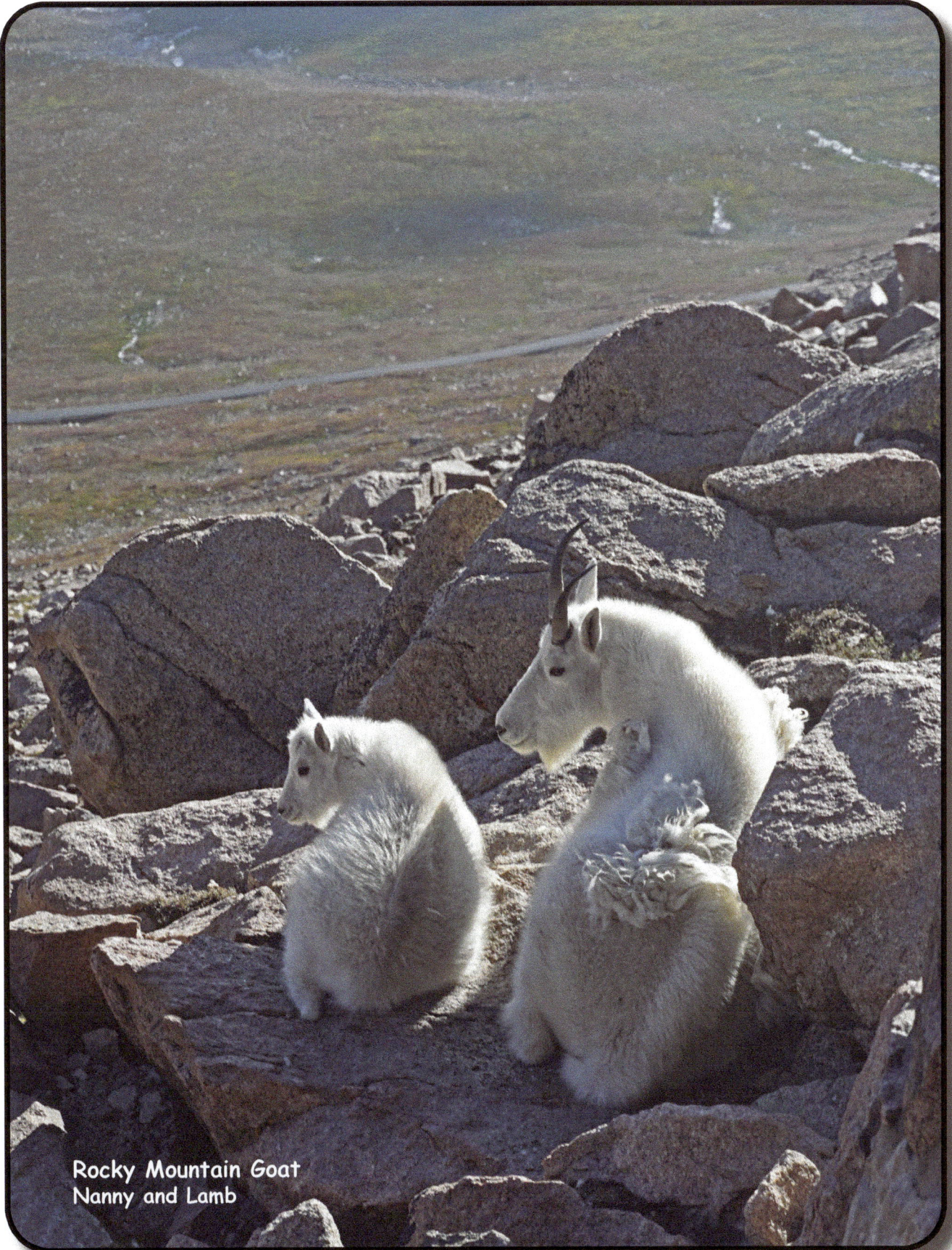

Rocky Mountain Goat
Nanny and Lamb

Yellow-bellied Marmot

Yellow-bellied Marmot

Moose, Cow

Moose, Cow
and Calf

Moose, Bull

Prairie Dog

Rabbit—Desert Cottontail

Raccoon

Big Horn Sheep
Rams and Ewes

Big Horn Sheep Herd

Big Horn Sheep Ram

Fox Squirrel

Fox Squirrel

REPTILES

Shown here are 4 species of reptiles in 4 photographs. On page 97 is a Painted Turtle sitting on a submerged Snapping Turtle. The State Reptile of Colorado is the Painted Turtle.

PLEASE
BRAKE

FOR

SNAKES

Red-eared Slider

Bull Snake

Bull Snakes
(mating)

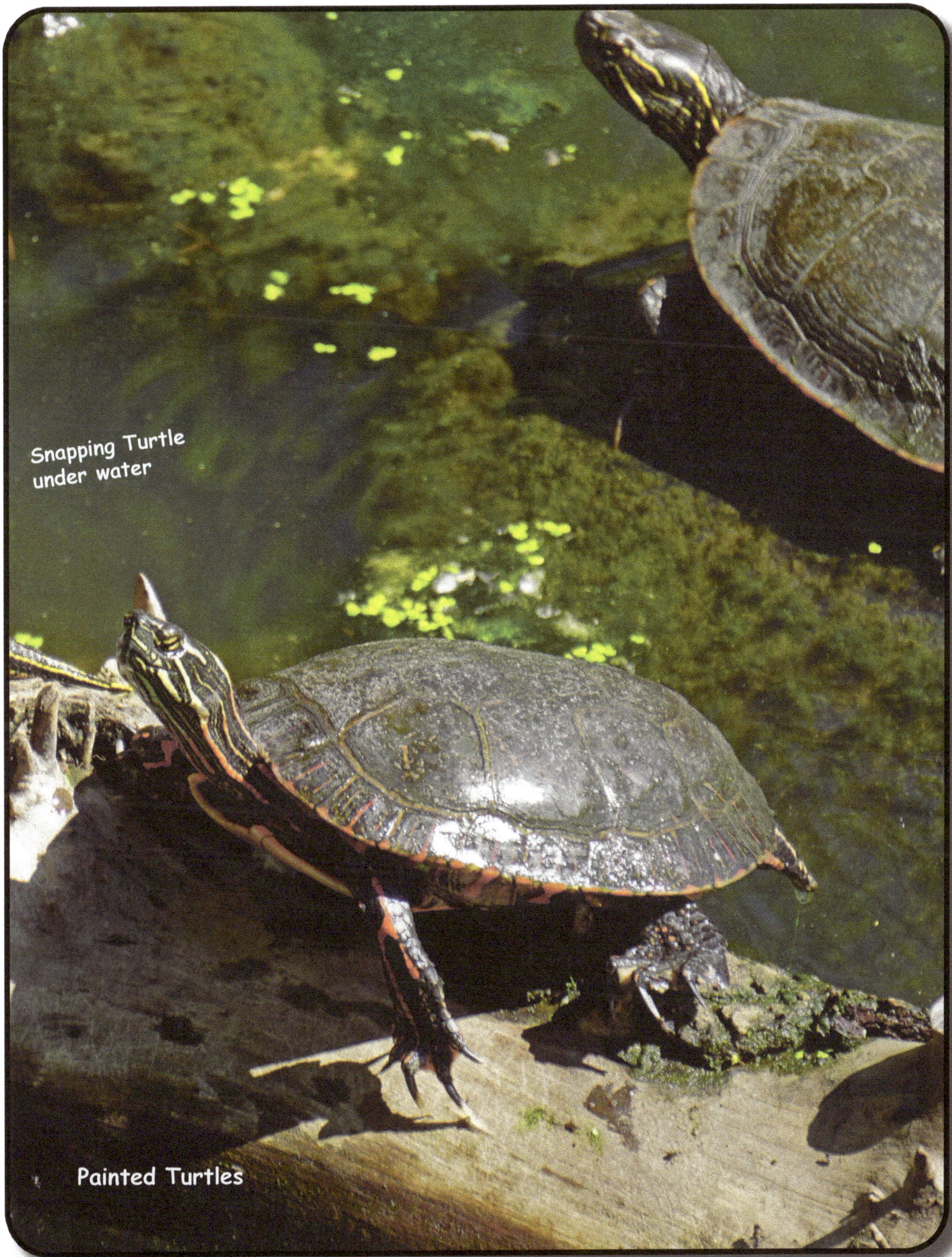
Snapping Turtle
under water
Painted Turtles

Last Words

If there are errors in identification in this collection then I take full responsibility. My primary reference sources are:

Sibley Birds West, © 2016, 2nd Edition, David Allen Sibley

Harper Collins Complete North American Wildlife, © 2003, 1st Edition, Gerard A. Bertrand, John A Burton and Paul Sterry.

Colorado Parks and Wildlife, https://cpw.state.co.us/ Managing 42 state parks, all of Colorado's wildlife, more than 300 state wildlife areas and a host of recreational programs.

About the Author

Photo credit: Bill Swanson

Joe McDaniel is a biologist, photographer and book publisher who has lived in Parker, Colorado, for over twenty years. He lived in Africa for twenty-five years and enjoys few things more than finding, observing and photographing wildlife. His wife, *Jan,* shares his interests and offers encouragement and a watchful eye. Each year they make a number of road trips to explore Colorado. Since 2007, Joe and Jan have owned their own small home-based business, **BookCrafters**, and have helped authors self-publish over 450 books.

They can be reached at bookcrafterscolorado@gmail.com.
or go to their website - http://bookcrafters.net

www.ingramcontent.com/pod-product-compliance
Lightning Source LLC
Chambersburg PA
CBHW042333030426
42335CB00027B/3316